Ethereum:

Ultimate Guide to Ether

Cryptocurrency, Blockchain Technology, Ethereum Virtual Machine, App Programming, Mining, Investing and Trading in Ethereum

Matthew Connor

Table of Contents

Introduction 5

Chapter 1: Introduction to Ethereum 7

Chapter 2: Blockchain Basics 20

Chapter 3: Money Making Basics 26

Chapter 4: Ethereum Mining.....................................44

Chapter 5: Ethereum Programing 49

Chapter 6: Smart Contracts 59

Chapter 7: Ethereum Tips and Tricks 64

Chapter 8: The Future of Ethereum 75

Conclusion 83

One Final Thing... 86

About The Author 87

Introduction

Congratulations on downloading **Ethereum: Ultimate Guide to Blockchain Technology, Cryptocurrency and Investing in Ethereum?**and thank you for doing so. The Ethereum platform takes all of the best parts of bitcoin and improves upon them using newer technology. Is it any wonder then that analysts are predicting the platform will have 100 times as many users in 2018 as it does in 2017?

In order to ensure that you are as up to date on the current technology trends as possible, the following chapters will discuss everything you need to know about Ethereum, including what it is doing to create a niche for itself in the crowded cryptocurrency marketplace. You will then learn a little bit about blockchain, the technology that powers the Ethereum platform. Next, you will get to the good stuff and start learning how to make money from investing in ether.

From there you will learn another way of profiting from the Ethereum platform, mining blocks. Then you will learn about the final major way to make money from the Ethereum platform, programming apps and smart contracts to work within the system. Finally, you will learn all about tips and tricks for success as well as what the future likely holds for Ethereum.

There are plenty of books on this subject on the market, thanks again for choosing this one! Every effort was made to ensure it is full of as much useful information as possible, please enjoy!

Chapter 1: Introduction to Ethereum

What is a Cryptocurrency?

A cryptocurrency is any type of digital currency that is based purely on computer code and gets its value from its use in the market as a whole rather than generating value by being a derivative of an existing asset. As an alternate option to traditional currencies, cryptocurrencies have become the new hot thing with investors over the past decade and it's easy to see why as they offer digital value that can be issued and tracked like their physical cousins.

Cryptocurrencies operate based on decentralized database technology which means that they can go through all their required processes successfully, day after day, without ever having to resort to an external authority to determine the next step. Blockchain is the most famous version of this technology, but there are several newer alternatives, like Ethereum that are aiming to give bitcoin a run for its money.

Decentralized cryptocurrencies have a wide variety of means for which to verify their transactions, the most common of these is a proof-of-work model. This is the model that creates the need for what are known as cryptocurrency miners one of the many ways that anyone can make a profit with cryptocurrency.

While traditional physical currencies are limited in a wealth of ways when it comes to deciding their worth, cryptocurrencies have no such hang ups and, thus, can range from anywhere from $.02 all the way up to bitcoin's market defying current price of $9780as of May 2018.

What is Ethereum?

Ethereum is currently one of the most popular cryptocurrency platforms on the market today. Its cryptocurrency is known as ether and it is mainly used for payment of services on the Ethereum platform which includes extensive use of what are known as smart contracts as well as the Ethereum Virtual Machine which allows users to generate decentralized apps that other users can then take advantage of in exchange for ether. Ether also see a fair amount of speculative investment, though it has not yet reached the heights of its main competitor bitcoin.

Ethereum was conceived of by a programmer associated with bitcoin by the name of Vitalik Buterin and written about in a whitepaper discussing decentralized applications in fall of 2013. His original pitch was to add a scripting language to bitcoin but his thoughts fell on deaf ears so he set out on his own to do just that. By the start of 2014, Buterin had his team together and by July 2015, Ethereum as we know it today was ready to launch.

In March of 2017, a wide variety of Fortune 500 companies, research groups and blockchain startups came together to form what is known as the Enterprise Ethereum Alliance. While it started with just 30 members, those numbers quickly swelled to over 100 in the first three months of operation. Notable names among the founding members list are JP Morgan, Intel, Microsoft, Samsung and more. The goal of the EEA is to generate a reference standard for the general Ethereum blockchain while also creating a variation of it that is permissioned to more easily address the common needs of businesses in a wide variety of industries.

Cryptocurrency of the future

Ethereum operates on an updated version of the blockchain code, discussed in detail in the next chapter, which is commonly referred to as blockchain 2.0. It offers improved transaction speeds as well as overall scalability and also makes it possible for each block in the blockchain to contain more complex code. This, in turn, has led to a much broader array of smart contracts than what bitcoin is currently able to provide. A smart contract is essentially a piece of code that will activate once specific external circumstances have been achieved. Once activated, the smart contracts can do things like making a trade or transferring funds between two accounts.

Smart contracts then tie back into the decentralized applications which are being created on the Ethereum platform as there are those that all for the facilitation of contract negotiation, with smart contracts taking care of all of the otherwise complicated financial transactions. These contracts are especially useful as the blockchain makes it easy to verify the transactions after the fact and also ensuring that neither party gets cold feet once the agreement has been made. This is not to say that smart contracts themselves will hold up in a court of law, they are only useful in enforcing otherwise legitimate legal documents.

Ethereum's publicly stated goal when it comes to promoting smart contracts is to decrease the standard cost of the fees associated with physical contracts by simplifying the cost as much as possible. While smart contracts are useful in a wide number of ways, they are still a fairly limited technology, at least for now. They will only work when it comes to binary actions, there is no room for gray when it comes to getting them to work properly. They are like light switches, they are either activated or not. Despite their limitations, smart contracts are already seeing a great deal of interest around the world as a way of issuing payments for copyrighted material in hopes of cutting down on piracy.

Digital tokens

Ethereum also provides users the ability to generate digital tokens that can represent a wide variety of things such as proofs of membership or virtual shares. These smart contract tokens can then be used in any standard ether wallet that uses the traditional API. These tokens can then be used to secure voting rights, as a means of fundraising or of simply indicating ownership shares in the company in question. Users can create either a predetermined number of tokens or create them on the fly as they are needed.

If created in large enough numbers, tokens can also be used as a means of generating additional funding for the company in question as a type of crowdfunding initiative. Entrepreneurs can then generate contracts asking for pledges from the community with all of the funds held in an account controlled by a smart contract until the target amount is reached. Each contract would then be presented by a token, which in turn would be worth a set amount of the new currency that would be created if the company gets off the ground.

Bitcoin versus Ethereum

Besides the increased reliance on smart contracts, Ethereum and bitcoin have other differences as well. The first of these is the rate of time which is required for new blocks to be created. With blockchain this process is currently capped at 10 minutes while Ethereum can manage it in just 12 seconds. This difference comes from what is known as the GHOST protocol which is a proprietary technology that allows for blocks to be confirmed much more quickly than they otherwise would. It does lead to a larger number of stalled blocks from time to time, however.

Another major difference is the amount of the cryptocurrency that is currently available to the public. An impressive 70 percent of all possible bitcoins have already been mined by those who got in on the concept on the ground floor. There are simply a finite number of bitcoins and this proportioning of the wealth is going to cause serious issues if it is not kept in check. On the other hand, less than 50 percent of all ether has already been minded which means the rest is still up for grabs.

This relative scarcity of bitcoins also leads to other effects, including the fact that the reward for mining bitcoins is essentially cut in half every four years, despite the required computations getting more complicated in the meantime. Compare this to the fact that the Ethereum platform is set up in such a way that each block is worth 5 ether, broken up by shares based on the work that was done to mine it.

The rate charged for transaction fees is also different between bitcoins and ether as the Ethereum platform utilizes a Gas system that determines the cost of individual transaction based on their bandwidth need, complexity and estimated storage. With bitcoin, transactions are inherently limited by the block size and every transaction competes equally with the next for validation.

When it comes to the speed at which both chains compute transactions, Ethereum uses what is known as a Turning complete internal code which means that given enough time virtually anything could be calculated. Bitcoin has more restrictions when it comes to the number of calculations it can process which means that its reach will eventually outpace its grasp. The Turning complete internal code isn't perfect, however, and it has led to additional security complications for Ethereum, including an attack in June 2017.

What is likely more important for those who are thinking about investing, while the blockchain chart is full of steep peaks and valleys, the ether price chart is much more bullish as of the

August 2017. Cryptocurrencies are social constructs when means they turn on robust networking effects. This, in turn, means that as long as the adoption rate of the Ethereum platform continues to increase then the utility of ether will continue to increase and its price will do the same.

This increase in usage is also worth keeping an eye for several other reasons. The first of these is the fact that the blockchain bitcoin runs off of is already working at its maximum capacity. The bitcoin blockchain can process about seven transactions each second but there are more than 3.5 million transactions that are waiting to be verified on average which means that even if no new transactions came through it would take the better part of a week to get through all the backlog. This is simply due to the case that the original blockchain code wasn't created to deal with this level of demand, it is nearly 10 years old after all.

This design flaw, coupled with the fact that smart contracts are easier to use on the Ethereum platform have lead many of the main developers in the blockchain space to switch their apps from one to the other. Ethereum's blockchain is optimized for a significantly higher number of transactions each second and the fees for each are lower besides. What all this really means is that the Ethereum platform is likely going to see a 10-fold increase in popularity by summer 2018 according to industry leading experts.

It may also be worth noting that many of the applications that are currently being built to run on the Ethereum platform are being done with an eye towards making the cryptocurrency process as easy to understand and simple to use as possible. As these projects come online, they are likely to expand the scope of the usage statistics even more. This then makes it much more likely to survive past the point where oversaturation hits the cryptocurrency market and culls the weakest from the heard. The Enterprise Ethereum Alliance is also a very positive sign that Ethereum is going to be around for the long-term.

Ethereum Virtual Machine (EVM)

The EVM, briefly touched on before, is the portion of the platform that is mainly focused on providing security and accessing trusted code with the help of computers and nodes all around the world. More specifically, it focuses on minimizing the likelihood of denial of service attacks occurring which are one of the most prevalent issues that plague cryptocurrency today. Additionally, the EVM works to minimize the chance that various programs can access the details of others while still providing pipelines for easy communication where appropriate.

More simply put, EVM is a virtual runtime environment that runs programs based on smart contracts and the Ethereum blockchain. It operates separately from the rest of the network which makes it the ideal testing environment as any company looking to generate a smart contract can easily do so in the EVM without having it affect their primary blockchain operations. Testing is clearly one of the most important steps of blockchain development as one line of flawed code is enough to render any smart contract useless.

It is also important to keep in mind that each instance of an Ethereum node also contains a version of the EVM which makes it an easy gateway to building more robust smart contracts for both veteran and novice coders. The Ethereum platform is based on the Solidity coding language and the EVM also primarily uses Python, Ruby and C++.

Ethereum pros and cons

When it comes to using Ethereum on a basic level it is a lot easier said than done, before you go through all of that trouble, it is important to consider the various pros and cons associated with the system before you start putting all of your eggs into an unreliable basket.

Pros

- Working with the Ethereum blockchain is a little like opening a franchise, it is relatively quick and easy to get started and create your own token, though of course you still need to know how to tell the token what to do.

- The Ethereum development team is hard at working always looking for ways to improve the existing platform. This means you can be confident that Ethereum's technology, along with its scalability, functionality, security and stability is going to continue to improve, at least for the time being.

- Not having to create your very own blockchain from scratch is going to save you lots of time and energy and using a variation of ether means that you know that at least someone will be using compatible cryptocurrency. You will also be able to launch your initial coin offering faster than you otherwise would, getting funding for your project more quickly than would otherwise be the case.

Cons

- Ethereum is more centralized than other blockchains which means that if the Ethereum network goes down, your service or cryptocurrency is going to go with it.

- Ethereum has hard forked before (created a secondary blockchain to combat fraud) and the results were wildly different for different people, some of whom experienced no change in their ether totals and others that found massive chunks of their savings missing. If you buy into Ethereum in a big way then you have to trust that such a scenario is unlikely to happen again.

- Not creating your own unique blockchain prevents you from having a say in the way your plans develop in the future. If you don't like the way Ethereum ultimately heads then it will be impossible for you to switch to a different platform without invalidating all of your user data during the conversion process. You would also destroy the cryptocurrency you created, essentially forcing you to start over from scratch.

- Improving functionality can be difficult as rather than simply working on your own blockchain you have to work on improving the Ethereum platform as a whole. Not only is this a much bigger job, you won't even see profitable results from most of your hard work.

- Ethereum based apps require gas to pay for their fees and gas goes to paying for the Ethereum network, not your own personal network. Having your own blockchain means you get to keep the fees that are associated with every transaction, something that will never happen if you choose to go with Ethereum.

Chapter 2: Blockchain Basics

If you are familiar with the term blockchain but don't really know how to explain it, don't worry, you aren't alone. Currently only about 25 percent of all Americans can accurately describe a blockchain, and only about 2 percent interact with the technology on a regular basis. As the name implies, blockchains are created from a score of individual blocks that each contain a variety of different details concerning their place in the chain along with the transaction data that is unique to them. When a new block is added to the chain from a single node, those details are then sent to all the other nodes that support the chain after verification of the data has occurred.

In addition to storing a wide variety of data types, each block also contains a timestamp to verify its place in the chain along with other classification data so its place in the chain can be determined automatically once it has been verified. This is only one way in which blockchain technology promotes autonomous completion of tasks which makes it truly decentralized. Once transactions are completed, they are collected at the nearest node while they are verified via an advanced cryptographic process. Once verification has occurred that information then spreads to the nodes closest to it before spreading out from there in an ease of use model.

Blockchain's security doesn't come from an outside source, rather it is a core part of the foundation of the system. If a transaction doesn't match what the blockchain as a whole expects it to be, then it is automatically deleted from the chain. This occurs thanks to a separate verification process that verifies the contents of the blockchain each time a node comes online. What this means is that in order to generate fraudulent activity, the fraudsters would need to generate the same false transactions across 51 percent or more of all nodes currently active at one time. The scale of such an attack means that the odds of it occurring are quite small, simply because the reward wouldn't justify the cost.

Blockchain components

Database

The primary difference between a blockchain database and a more traditional database is the ideal level of centralization required. The average conventional database tries to ensure the greatest level of centralization possible in order to ensure maximum efficiency when it comes to data transmission.

Decentralized databases give up that need for speed in exchange for a system that can function worldwide. When this node based structure is combined with the unique security options at play in the blockchain technology, coupled with the fact that it can easily sort data automatically, what you get is a form of banking that is as secure as it is autonomous. Blockchains essentially transfer currencies in the same way that the internet as a whole processes information.

Hashes

Stored blockchain data can be broken into two types, the data in the block and the data about the block. A majority of the data is going to concern individual transactions from people moving their cryptocurrency around, the rest is created once the block is verified. At this point, the block's information, along with the information about the block itself is encrypted via a process known as a hash function. This means that even if a hacker accessed a blockchain's records, they wouldn't see all of the specific transaction records, they would see the blockchain's hash function which is, more or less, a digital fingerprint.

Changing just one character of this code can alter or corrupt the data in unexpected ways, so without the proper key, the data is practically worthless. The most commonly used hash function is SHA-256. Data that is encrypted using this function can only be decoded if they have access to the decryption key that was made for it expressly. Each block of the chain is given a unique hash code at the time of verification, as are each of the transactions inside it. This hash is then modified based on the block's ultimate location in the chain as a whole and its neighbors. If the details for a block don't match those of the surrounding blocks then the new block won't make it into the chain.

Merkle trees

A Merkle tree is a process that makes it much easier for blockchains to run in the decentralized way that is their trademark. It is basically a functionality matrix that allows the verification process to proceed as quickly as possible. It also makes it easier for vast financial transactions to be broken into chunks which are easier to digest which makes it possible for users to follow the follow the flow of the trade data as easily as possible. The Merkle tree is also a critical part of the security protocols of the blockchain and while it is possible to build one without the other, those versions tend to be slower and less secure than the preferred version.

After a block has been added to the chain, its hashes are then combined with the hashes of the adjacent blocks, these hashes are then combined with other hashes and so on and so forth until the whole blockchain has one interconnected hash that is updated with each new block. This hash is known as the root hash and it is at the heart of the Merkle tree's usefulness. Also known as a Merkle root, it can be thought of as the sum total of all of the individual hashes that are a part of it. The Merkle tree can then easily verify the data of a given block through its relation to the Merkle root as a whole. Each time a new block is added, the tree as a whole verifies the data of each block is where it should be and the integrity of the chain is confirmed.

The Merkle tree got its name due to the way that it processes information. As it checks the data available at the moment, it creates branches that split off in a factor of two, this allows the tree to verify the data in question without compromising the data in the chain as a whole. If the information doesn't match with the data in the prime timeline then it can be easily expelled. At each point, the new information that is stored in a particular block is given one branch and the primary data is given another. The Merkle tree then verifies that all the correct hashes are in place, rather than reverifying all of the data bit by bit and makes a decision from there.

Manually verifying this amount of data would be a colossal task that, if performed by people, would make blockchain transactions an impossibility. The Merkle tree simplifies this process and also limits the amount of data that individual nodes would need to share at any given time, which speeds up the process even more. Every time that a particular hash is flagged in multiple locations, it is checked and double checked for accuracy across corresponding nodes.

Chapter 3: Money Making Basics

Investing in ether

2016 was the year the cryptocurrency market really exploded and now there are various types of all shapes and sizes floating around in the investment markets. While bitcoin still has the greatest price and the largest trading volume, Ethereum still saw a respective 300 percent growth last year. This doesn't mean that investing in ether is without risk, however, which is why it is important to keep in mind the pros and cons outlined here prior to making any investment decisions.

Little chance of fraud

As ether is an all-digital currency, it makes it much more difficult for it to be affected by fraud in the traditional sense. They cannot be forged or counterfeited and once a transaction has been verified it is in the blockchain forever and cannot be reversed.

Furthermore, they offer paramount protection when it comes to preventing identity theft when compared to more traditional exchanges. While traditional exchanges require a steady stream of charges to your debit card or checking account to fund the process. If you are using cryptocurrency to buy cryptocurrency, however, you frequently don't need to even verify any information, just plug in your wallet details and get to work. Getting rid of this step means there are infinitely fewer ways for unscrupulous individuals to get at your money.

Unlimited access

More than 2.5 billion people worldwide have ready access to the internet but not to a traditional banking establishment. This means that cryptocurrencies like ether have a very large, and very eager, target audience just waiting for the technology to become mainstream. As such, moving forward, more and more business is going to take place exclusively through digital mediums which means that those who invest early are more likely to see a dramatic increase in overall value, possibly sooner rather than later. While you may still be hesitant, consider this, more Kenyans have access to a bitcoin wallet than either clean water or indoor plumbing. Cryptocurrencies are on the verge of breaking out in a big way and Ethereum is poised to be at the center of the action.

Lower costs

While every ether transaction is going to cost you a little

bit of gas to facilitate the process, the fact of the matter is that buying into a given position on ether is almost always going to cost you less than if you when through a traditional brokerage for a traditional long or short transaction. Cryptocurrencies have fewer hoops to jump through than the traditional forms of currency and the price for individual trades reflects that.

Uncertain future

While bitcoin has proved to be a winning investment for the past eight years, and Ethereum has grown year over year since its inception, despite some down times in-between, that doesn't mean that this is going to continue to be the case in the long-term. There simply isn't enough past data to say with any real degree of certainty what the market is going to look like a year from now, much less 5 or 10 which means that both the potential for loss and the potential for gain are virtually limitless. Basically, what this means is that up until the time that the cryptocurrency market stabilizes, any dollar you put into Ethereum is just as likely to be worth more next year than it is today as it is to be completely worthless.

Large amount of volatility

Due to its unstable nature, the cryptocurrency market is one of the most volatile places to invest, leading to bigger losses just as frequently as it leads to big gains. As an example, bitcoin is by far the most stable of all of the cryptocurrencies on the market today and it is still five times less stable than gold and six times more volatile than the stocks on the S&P 500. Also adding to the high degree of volatility is the fact that a majority of all cryptocurrency transactions, and 80 percent of all ether transactions, are purely speculative which means that it is just investors trying to get in before the next big jump in price. This is important to keep in mind as it likely means that the price is currently in a bubble which can't sustain itself forever.

No physical backup

While the fact that ether and other cryptocurrencies aren't directly tied to anything in the physical world is obviously one of their biggest selling points, it does have its drawbacks as well. Specifically, it is important to keep in mind that any ether that you buy is only going to exist in your Ethereum wallet, and if that wallet malfunctions for any reason then you could easily lose the only record you have of the cryptocurrency in your possession.

Additionally, the sheer potential for profit that the cryptocurrency exchanges represent means that hackers are always going to be on the lookout for security weaknesses that are potentially exploitable. Don't forget, the Ethereum platform has been attacked numerous times over the years and one of the attacks was so successful that an entirely new chain had to be created as a response. There is now an Ethereum Classic blockchain as well as the standard Ethereum blockchain for just this reason. Hard forks such as this one could literally never happen in the real world and truly shows how potentially hazardous trading ether can be.

Ether Trading

Cryptocurrency trading can be a profitable means of investing regardless of how familiar you are with securities trading as a whole. It is also very easy to get started with as well, and requires little more than finding a reliable exchange, making a deposit and placing the trade. If you already have cryptocurrency in your possession, for one reason or another, then you likely won't even need to verify your account.

Another perk is the fact that all the various cryptocurrency exchanges aren't connected which means their pricing is based on the movement their traders are generating which, in turn, leads to larger spreads. It also leads to scenarios where you can pick up a currency on one exchange and immediately turn around and sell it for a profit on another. This lack of overall regulation also means that the potential for large margins is in place which makes the cryptocurrency market the place to go if you want to turn a small stack into a large stack, as long as you can handle the risk.

As previously mentioned, ether is currently in the midst of a price bubble which will continue to increase as long as people keep buying into it. While this won't help those, who buy in once the bubble is well-established, it is very useful for those who got in early as long as they don't overstay their welcome and sell before the boom cycle becomes a bust cycle.

When it comes to trading ether through trading companies, the most common means of doing so is through what are known as contracts for differences. These types of agreements allow the seller and the buyer to come to an agreement that says the buyer will pay the seller the difference between the price of an asset when the contract was signed and a predetermined period of time, assuming the price movement is positive. If the price movement is negative, then the seller would pay out the buyer the difference instead.

When it comes to maximizing leverage, rates of 20 to 1 are relatively easy to find so every $1 you put into an investment could actually get you $20 back, per unit of the ether that you purchase. While this will obviously lead to a serious profit in some cases, if you lose you will need to pay back $20 for every $1, which mitigates the benefits in some instances.

Other benefits

Worldwide currency

When it comes to traditional physical currencies, they are generally limited when it comes to external changes that can alter their price on the currency market. This is not the case with ether, and indeed all cryptocurrencies, however, as anything in the world has the potential to affect prices based solely on the way that investors react because of it. For example, bitcoin saw some of its most serious moves when the Chinese government decreased the value of the yuan or when new capital controls went into effect in Greece.

Constant access

Unlike other markets, the cryptocurrency market never closes which means that if you have a hankering to own some new ether at 3 am Sunday morning then all you have to do is log on to your cryptocurrency exchange of choice and see what trades are ready and waiting. Furthermore, there are currently more than 100 different exchanges, each with their own rates and trading trends which means it should be relatively easy to find the sort of trade you are looking for.

This constant level of access also serves to increase volatility as anything happening anywhere has the possibility to cause a drop in confidence levels that can set off a serious swing in the price of a specific cryptocurrency. Ether and the other major cryptocurrencies often see swings of five percent or more each day and the smaller currencies routinely swing as much as 15 percent each day.

Set up an ether wallet

Before you can get started making money trading ether you are going to need to set up a cryptocurrency wallet. Much like a physical wallet holds cash, your cryptocurrency wallet is going to hold all of your ether or any other cryptocurrency you may choose to purchase. While any old wallet will hold your physical cash, it is important to give your ether wallet a little more thought as it is all that stands between your coins and someone else's pocket. As such, there are several different types of wallets available, all of which have their own strengths and drawback.

The most frequently used type of cryptocurrency wallet is the online variety which can be accessed online or via apps for tablets or smartphones. A majority of these are multisystem as well so they will work with multiple operating systems. If, on the other hand, you are willing to give up some ease of use in exchange for extra security then you are going to want to look into a hardware wallet. A hardware wallet is an encrypted USB drive that will store your coins and ensure that you are the only one who has access to them. Each type of hardware wallet is going to be OS specific. Finally, if you want to use your ether to purchase things in the real world then you might be interested in a paper wallet. A paper wallet is a wallet that is stored on a computer without internet access that is also connected to a printer so you can print off an ever-changing wallet code to hand to individuals to pay for your transactions.

Choosing the best exchange possible

When it comes to actually giving your money, and possibly even access to your checking account, to some website you heard about online it is important to do as much research as possible beforehand to keep yourself from making a huge mistake. Remember, there is very little preventing your exchange from just packing it in one day and calling it quits, taking your money with it. What's more, if this happens you are likely not going to have much chance of getting it back in the first place. This is where transparency is going to start playing a larger role as you are going to want to find the most transparent exchange possible.

First you are going to want to take at the exchange's order book, which is a complete recording of everything that the exchange has done since it has been on the market. You should also be able to find out a wide variety of information including what their reserve currency levels are like and where they keep the fund's fund. If you can't track down this information, and the exchange you are using isn't completely brand new then they are keeping information from you, and likely not for an especially positive reason.

The most common of these is that the exchange is actually what is known as a fractional exchange because they only keep a fraction of the money required to square their debts available at one time. This, in turn, means that if there is ever a serious run on the cryptocurrency in question then it won't be able to fulfill its obligations and will likely fold as a result.

General strength of security

Outside of transparency, the next most important thing that you are going to want to look for in a good exchange is the level of security that they are making use of. At the minimum, you are going to want an exchange that starts with HTTPS and not just HTTP. This means the site is operating under a secure protocol which means the odds of your account details being stolen is going to dramatically decrease. It is also important to choose one that provides two-factor authentication and enforces strict login practices. If you end up choosing an exchange that doesn't offer these security basics then you are leaving yourself open to the possibility of identity theft at a later point and time.

Check out the fees

It doesn't matter if you are buying ether or another, less popular cryptocurrency, you are going to need to pay the fees your exchange puts in place, in addition to a small fee from the platform that you are using, to fund their services as well. Part of that fee is going to go directly to the person who is verifying your transaction in the first place. While, in many cases, these fees are strictly voluntary, if you don't pay them upfront then those who are mining blocks are going to be much less inclined to mine your block specifically. This, in turn, means that you would need to wait much longer to receive your money than you otherwise would. Chinese exchanges typically do not charge additional fees on top of what the platform is already charging. Not taking fees into account can start eating into your profits surprisingly quickly and is not recommended.

Choose a local exchange if possible

While not all countries are going to have a cryptocurrency exchange that trades in ether, it is a good idea to always choose an exchange that is as close to your home country as possible. Not only will it make it easier for you to file a complaint if your exchange does something shady, and even increase the odds that you might get your money back if this occurs, it will help you see larger profits as well. This is the case because the exchange will naturally see increased periods of trading on a schedule that you can more easily take advantage of than if your exchange is most active when it is the middle of the night in your part of the world.

It is also important to look into the types of currencies that your chosen exchange deals in, even if they are local, as this is no guarantee they are going to deal in the currency pair you are interested in. USD is without a doubt the most commonly used base currency, even in China, which means if that you are looking for something else you will need to do some extra research.

Length of transaction time

As cryptocurrency transactions need to be verified before they go through, cryptocurrency exchanges are going to work on a lead time to give these verifications the time they need to happen. This means you are going to need to be aware of the amount of time your chosen exchange is going to hold onto your money before you can expect anything to happen. Along similar lines, you are going to want to choose an exchange that locks in the details of a trade right away, as opposed to waiting for the transaction to be verified first. If this is not the case, then your trading percentages could be off simply because a trade slipped between when you placed a trade and when it actually went through.

Popular Ethereum exchanges

Kraken

This is one of the top 15 most popular exchanges that trades in USD and is also the most popular exchange that deals in euros. It also offers a number of smaller cryptocurrencies for trading, though only in limited trading pairs.

Coinbase

This the longest lasting cryptocurrency exchange that has been in continuous operation on the market today. It is extremely well regulated and is one of the top five exchanges with the highest daily volume.

OKCoin

This exchange is great for those who are looking for fewer

regulations, but still want to trade USD. This exchange is based in China so most of the rules that traditionally govern exchanges do not apply.

Bitstamp

This is another elder statesman of the cryptocurrency exchanges, having first opened in 2011. It is the second most popular exchange and sees more than 10,000 trades every day.

Bitfinex

With more than 200,000 trades a week, Bitfinex is the most popular cryptocurrency exchange on the market today. This is an exchange that lets you trade without verification if you already have cryptocurrency in hand.

Initial Coin Offering

These days, investing in cryptocurrency, especially those based on the Ethereum platform, via initial coin offerings is becoming an increasingly common occurrence. In 2017, one new cryptocurrency known as Bancor, raised nearly $200 million in one day and others have hit half that amount in the same period in time. In fact, 2017 has seen ICOs raise more than $500,000,000 for a wide variety of cryptocurrencies so far.

While initial coin offering is a play on the term initial public offering, ICOs and IPOs are dramatically different things. An ICO is essentially just a crowdfunding strategy that blockchain-based businesses can use as a means of funding the startup phase of their business plan. This is an especially common strategy on the Ethereum Platform as it is so easy for individuals to create their own tokens, that are then given out to those who buy in at a rate that is theoretically going to be worth less than the value of the currency once everything shakes out. Those who invest early are then essentially betting the market that the cryptocurrency in question is going to be useful enough to find an audience that uses it for something besides speculation. This sort of usage will maximize demand and ensure the price rises enough to make the initial investment a good deal.

A majority of ICO funding seems to be coming from China these days, though investors from across the globe have been known to jump in on the ground floor if the price is right. Besides the conventional wisdom that goes along with investing in an untested commodity, ICOs have their own issues which make them extra risky. The biggest of these is the fact that the Securities and Exchange Commission is currently looking into whether ICOs are avoiding regulations that would require them to have to meet the same standards as IPOs. There is also a fear that the current round of ICO success has created a bubble around the market that can only be sustained for so long.

Regardless of their potential concerns, ICOs have still proved to be a significant source of profits for investors who buy into them at the right time. Either way, if you plan on looking into ICO investment then you will want to keep in mind that if investing in cryptocurrency is risky, then investing in ICOs is risky enough to make investing in cryptocurrency look mundane.

It also means that investing in an ICO successfully means approaching it with an analytical mindset. You will need to start by looking into any documentation that may be available from the company, most importantly a business plan or the closest thing they can come up with as an equivalent. This is crucial as it will allow you to determine if the project you might be funding ultimately makes sense from a practical standpoint and will thus be more likely to find success in both the short and the long-term. It is also important that you take the time to consider if there is already a proven demand for the product or service that the company is going to provide. Finally, it is important that the cryptocurrency you are buying into is going to be a key part of that business plan, not just something to give to early investors.

Furthermore, you will need to keep in mind that buying into an ICO doesn't provide you with many of the benefits of an

IPO. Buying into an ICO doesn't give you any of the ownership rights that buying into an IPO does, you are essentially just buying the cryptocurrency in question on the cheap. IPO are required to meet certain standards when it comes to accreditation and fiduciary obligations and ICOs are not.

As a general rule, ICOs run light which means you may be lucky to see a business plan, a website and a whitepaper on their concept, and sometimes not even all of these. As they are rarely ever going to have an actual product ready to demo, you will need to take their pitch on faith which means you are raising the level of risk significantly when compared to most other investment scenarios. It is critical to point out that just because an ICO goes well, doesn't mean that public opinion on the company in general is going to remain strong. In fact, many venture capitalists believe that getting too much money, too fast, is actually detrimental to new companies as management often feels the need to spend what they have without dedicating the right amount of time to actually generating a strong product. All in all, it may make more sense to wait to see if any of the current round of ICOs find success before making this type of investment.

Finally, it is important to keep in mind that the sheer fact that all of these companies are creating their blockchain products on the Ethereum platform which means that their initial investments costs were likely quite low. This means it is very possible that they could cut their losses at any point, at least until they become a bit more established. At the same time, this is a strong vote of confidence in Ethereum by the masses as the platform that promotes the new technology the most effectively typically sticks around for the long-term.

Chapter 4: Ethereum Mining

While the mining of bitcoin is all the rage in certain sectors these days, the cryptocurrency king isn't the only one of its kind to utilize the help of the masses when it comes to verifying transactions. Rather, every cryptocurrency that uses a proof-of-work model uses more or less the same process. Mining is accomplished via the use of high powered computers, or mining machines, that use a version of the SHA-256 mining process in order to uphold the sanctity and security of the blockchain. The speed with which a given machine can validate transactions is determined in hashes per second.

In exchange for mining on the Ethereum platform, you will receive ether to offset your costs and hopefully help you to turn a profit. Each ether is worth a little over $300, and each mined block rewards a total of 5 ether to the group of individuals who mined it. You will also receive a portion of the gas fees that are charged to fund the process as well. The more powerful the machine you use to mine blocks, the more you will ultimately make in mining fees.

The most frequently used proof-of-work validation is called the hashcash proof-of-work and it is an algorithm which utilizes the hash as a core part of the process. Hashcash proofs can then be tweaked for individual difficulty to make sure that there are not blocks being generated at a rate that is faster than what the network can realistically handle. This is where the limitation on transactions per second that bitcoin struggles with comes from. The overall probability of being chosen for the next generation is quite low which makes guessing which mining machine is going to get the next block a very difficult proposition.

In order for a new block to be perceived as valid, the hash value it shows need to be greater than that of the one before it which means the block naturally includes the work that was put into generating it. Each block then also contains the hash of the proceeding block which determines where it belongs in the chain as a whole. This means that a block can only ever be changed if the work done on all previous blocks is altered as well.

Getting started

The best mining hardware and the price for the same are always going to be changing, which means the best place to go for up to date information is going to be the Ethereum subreddit. You should be able to easily find out the current state of the market as well as what hardware is currently considered state of the art. A wide variety of premade and made to order mining machines can be found on Amazon.com. The cost for these systems runs from $500 to $4,500 or more.

Regardless of the type of system you choose to go with, you are going to need dedicated hardware in order to mine effectively. While you may be able to technically mine using your computer's video card or your laptop's CPU, specialized mining machines are always going to outpace you if this is the case, stealing any verifications out from under you before you even got started. The most popular chips in these machines are made by ASIC and are generally about 100 times faster than the average computer. Trying to mine without having the right hardware in place will generally just end up costing you more time and money than the entire endeavor is worth.

Getting online

After you have a mining machine ready and waiting, you will then need to download the program that you will use to automate the mining process. There are several different versions of this type of program available, the most commonly used ones are BFGminer, EasyMiner and CGminer, of these, EasyMiner is the only one that uses a standard graphical interface, the others run via command line prompts.

Connect to a pool

Once you have the required software and hardware, the next thing you will need to do is to join an ether mining pool. A mining pool is a confederation of miners who band together with the goal of verifying larger blocks more quickly than what could be done by each alone. The rewards for doing so are then shared evenly among the miners who helped with the verification. While this step is strictly optional, you will likely find far more blocks to mine as part of a pool than you will by your lonesome. This is due to the fact that the amount of computational power required for the average verification these days is far beyond the means of what most machines can do in a reasonable period of time.

If you decide to strike out on your own then you will need to download the Ethereum core client to keep your machine in sync with the Ethereum blockchain. This client can be downloaded from Ethereum.org. Assuming you decide to go with a mining pool instead, then all you will need to do is follow the instructions of the leader of the pool instead.

Choosing the right pool for you will likely be a challenge, simply because there are going to be so many different ones to choose rom. The best way to determine the best options for you is by researching user feedback from each and choosing the best one from there. Joining up with an extremely popular pool means that you will have the chance to get in on more verifications while going with a smaller pool means that your individual shares from each verification are likely going to be larger.

Chapter 5: Ethereum Programing

In order to create your own app on the Ethereum platform, you are going to want to use the Solidity programing language which is similar to JavaScript. It uses both the .sol and the .se extension in addition to LLL, the byproduct of Lisp. If you have even used Python or Serpent then Solidity is sure to feel familiar and users from both are switching to Solidity on a regular basis.

In order to easily compile the apps and smart contracts that you create, you will need to use a variation of the solc compiler that uses C++. If you prefer not to go the solc route, you can instead use a browser based alternative such as Cosmo, though this chapter will assume you went with the solc complier. Furthermore, once you have compiled your work you are going to need to use the Ethereum Web3.ja API in order to utilize the JavaScript that will connect the smart contract to the app. This will ultimately allow you to interact with your smart contracts directly without forcing you to log into an Ethereum node to do so.

Distributed application framework

There are several different frameworks that have already been created by likeminded developers that have been released to the Ethereum community for free with the goal of improving community output as a whole. One of these is a great place to start without having to worry about building your own framework from the ground up.

Embark/Truffle

Truffle is a great framework to start with as it automates several of the more generic steps in the programming process as a means of developing distributed applications more readily by providing developers more free time to work on deploying, compiling and testing the best code they can manage. Embark typically comes in handy when building and streamlining apps by automating much of the testing process.

Meteor

When it comes to improving the stack, Meteor, which naturally works with the Web3.js API, is the choice of many Ethereum developers. It also works as a standard web application framework as well. Meteor is one of the leading supporters of the Ethereum platform as was discussed heavily at the November 2016 Ethereum Development Conference.

APIs

The most common decentralized API is that which was created by BlockApps.net. It mimics a normal Ethereum node if you are not in a position to run a real one at the moment. A common alternative is called MetaMask which makes it easy to run the standard array of Ethereum platform tools on any web browser. Another option is LightWallet which is an easy way for users and developers to interact with decentralized apps with different interfaces for each group of users.

Build your own app

1. The first thing you will need to do in order to create an app successfully is to create an Ethereum node to work from. The best way to go about doing so is through Geth, the Ethereum node interface.

   a. From the command line, enter
      bash<(curlhttps://install-geth.ethereum.org)

   b. Next you will be prompted to begin the Geth installation, you will need to select the appropriate operating system along with the latest version of the

Ethereum CLL.

c. After the installation has completed successfully, you will then be free to interact with Geth through an environment based on JavaScript along with standard console commands. Specialized console commands will be saved between instances in order to allow you to track your progress more easily.

d. All that is left at this point is to get to work. Open a terminal tool as a means of opening the Geth console. After the program launches you should see a less than sign as an indication that things are working properly. To quit, you simply type exit at that point and press the ENTER key.

e. The Geth console will automatically redirect or log output to the console if you use the command gethconsole2>>geth.log. You will also be able to access this log via the command tail-fgeth.log.

2. The next thing you are going to do, after creating the smart contract or decentralized application in question, is to compile it using the solc C++ compiler.

3. Once everything has been compiled, you will now be

ready to deploy your results. In order to do so you are going to need to pay a gas fee and also digitally sign a contract. After this is done you will then receive access to a specific address that houses the contract in the blockchain as well as the ABI for your new product.

4. Once you have the ABI you will then be able to check on the contract or application from any device that is connected to the internet. Depending on what your creation does exactly, each time you interact with it you may need to pay a gas fee.

Testing

If you are creating a smart contract then it is important that your if/then statements are constructed in such a way that there is no room for questioning whether or not specific qualifications are met. This is where Truffle comes into play as it will automatically generate the type of framework that JavaScript and Web3.js need in order to make this type of code work correctly.

Test the transaction time

The promises that you decide to utilize are going to be a crucial part of whether your smart contract or app actually sees use as it is going to take at least 10 seconds for your contract to be verified, and that is just the speed that is attainable under perfect testing conditions. When you are ready to begin testing your contract you are going to need to head to the test directory and change the extension on the .js file to conference.js and also change any other references as well. After this, all you are going to need to do is run Truffle in the root directory that holds your test file. With this done you will then:

1. Begin by opening Pip, Solidity and solc. You will want to ensure your main library is separated from your test library by using a virtual environment.

2. Once this is done you are going to need to open the console window and start a new node client. You will need to start Truffle and then use the deploy command to activate the standard init that can be used with smart contracts. Doing so will also allow the program to point out any errors that the code may contain at this point.

3. As you develop your code, it is always a good idea to test the compilation in Truffle to ensure that you aren't taken by surprise when you go to compile the final version. Truffle will also allow you to test the deployment of contracts in a test space as well.

Deployment

Once you have successfully tested your contract you can then deploy it from Truffle directly. In order to go about doing so:

1. Start by opening the console and using the code truffle init (new directory) to generate a new directory.

2. Locate the contract you have created, it will be listed as name.solc.

3. Open the app.json/config file and type in the name of your new contract under the space for Contracts.

4. Start up your Ethereum node, open another window in the console before using the tesrpc command.

5. With that done you will then need to run Truffle again and choose the option to deploy from the root directory.

Relevant variables for smart contracts

The variables that you add to a smart contract are always going to be organized in the same fashion.

The first variable will be the address variable which refers to the location of the ether wallet that is going to be the primary account for the contract. This address is generated when the contract is created and can be found via the conference () function. The address will either be listed as the owner's or the organizer's wallet. If you use Geth, you will have the ability to generate different account addresses from a single node. If you are using this feature then the address variable is always going to refer to the primary account that is created. Every smart contract that is created will have a pair of addresses, the first being the wallet address and the second is the address of the contract after it is deployed. You can gain access to the contract address directly via the primary Solidity interface through the command contract: address myaddress=this.

The second variable in the UINIT variable which is an abbreviation for unsigned integer. This variable is generally listed as 256.

The third variable is going to be either PRIVATE OR PUBLIC which will determine if the smart contract you have created is going to be able to access information outside the blockchain directly through the use of what is known as an oracle. If outside information is required then this will be set to public, otherwise private will suffice.

The next two variables are ARRAYS and MAPPING which Solidity will automatically generate details for. In order to change these presets, you will need to use the command address=>unit. You will need to make sure that your overall contract footprint and any related information is as small as possible. These variables are ultimately used to determine who has to pay for what after specific variables are achieved.

Suicide button

It is important to always include a suicide option in your smart contracts that will allow them to self-destruct when needed. This is important if you accidentally make a mistake and a transfer doesn't go through properly then the only way to get the transaction out of limbo is to destroy the contract and start again. Once destroyed, the funds will return to their primary wallet.

Calls

A call function is a call that changes the way the current contract operates through modifying existing records or adding new records to an exciting set. This can also be done through the Web3.js function as it can be used to move variables around in a specific smart contract. These variables can be determined beforehand through the use of Solidty, more specifically the msg.sender and msg.value commands. Altering either of the resulting variables will alter where the funds are coming from and how much will reach the account designated to receive them.

Events

Depending on the ultimate use of the smart contract in question, it will need to include various events including receiving or sending funds that will be listed in the events log section of the smart contract that can be found connected to the block that the transaction ends up being attached to. This variable won't change what the smart contract is up to, it just makes all the details easier to reference.

Chapter 6: Smart Contracts

When it comes to making the most out of smart contracts, the front lines these days are on the Ethereum Platform. While the Bitcoin platform is, first and foremost, a means of facilitating cryptocurrency transactions, Ethereum is heavily focused in the area of smart contract technology and a majority of its applications run some type of smart contract or another.

Mapping: A mapping is a type of associative array that associates balances and addresses. These addresses are then stored in the common hexadecimal format, while the balances are converted to integers ranging somewhere between 0 and 115 quattuorvigintillion. If the mapping includes the public keyword, then the variable in question will be visible by everyone on the blockchain. This is crucial in order for clients to display them properly.

MyToken: If you published your contract immediately, it would attempt to use available coins, but at the same time would be unable to find any. As such, in order to make the contract useful, you need to create a few tokens as well. This can be done with the MyToken function by changing the balanceOf variable to something greater than zero. The function is based on the contract MyToken which means that if you change the name of the contract you will need to change the name of the function in order to ensure things continue working properly. This function then sets the balance to the determined amount in the account of the user who deployed the contract in the first place.

When you are creating your smart contract in the Ethereum platform, you can accomplish much the same thing from the drop-down menu on the right hand side of the screen. There you will find the "pick a contract" option which holds a option for MyToken. Within that option you will then find a section known as constructor parameters which offer numerous parameters for your token including the initial supply and the transaction fee.

Transfer function: The transfer function is very straightforward, it has a value that serves as a parameter as well as a recipient and when it is used it then subtracts the relevant _value from one balance and adding it to another. The biggest issue that needs to be addressed from a coding perspective is the way in which users are prevented from sending more _value than their existing balance allows for. To mitigate this issue you will need to include a check that guarantees the sender has enough funds to execute the transaction otherwise it is stopped. This method also serves to prevent overflows which will prevent a number from getting so large that it rolls back over to zero.

A contract can be canceled mid-execution through the use of either a throw or return. A return tends to cost less but is also more of a hassle as it cancels out of the contract but keeps any changes that the contract received in the interim. As such, the throw command is typically cleaners as it reverts changes to transaction that could have been made, though it does cause the user to lose any gas they have put into the transaction. It will also generate a warning that this will occur to the user, however, making the loss on them if they go through with it.

Deploying a contract: Once you have completed your contract, you will need to deploy it in order for it to do much of anything. To do so, you will want to use the token source code outlined above, open your Ethereum Wallet and then paste the code into the source field for Solidity. Assuming the code compiles properly, you will then see the option to pick a contract from the right drop down menu. You will then be able to select the contract labeled MyToken. You will then be given the option to personalize your token a little more.

At the bottom of the screen you will be presented with an estimate as to the cost of the contract you are creating, in general the default settings should be sufficient. Pressing deploy will set tings in motion and ensure you are redirected to the front page where you should see your transaction waiting to be confirmed. Choosing the name of your primary account will then transfer 100 percent of the shares of the new token to that account.

You will then be able to send your currency to anyone whose Ethereum wallet address that you have access to as any Ethereum wallet will naturally be able to store tokens created through the blockchain as well. This does not, however, mean that the wallet will detect the new cryptocurrency automatically, however as this detail has to be added in manually. It can be found under the tab labeled Contracts where a link should be visible that will take the user to the freshly minted contract. You will then want to copy the address into your text editor.

To add the token to the wallet's watch list, you will go back to the contract page before selecting the option to Watch Token. This will present you with a pop-up box that will appear, into which you will need to paste the contract address. This, in turn, will fill in the name of the token, its symbol and its decimal number. Any details changed here will only reflect how the token is viewed in the wallet, not anything about the currency itself. With this done, the wallet will then display the number of tokens that are currently available and allow interaction with them as normal.

Chapter 7: Ethereum Tips and Tricks

Avoid fraud

Because of the fact that the cryptocurrency market is essentially unregulated, it is important that you protect yourself if you want to avoid being the victim of fraud. Rest assured, scammers are out there looking to take advantage of any means necessary to separate you from your hard-earned ether. Below you will find a variety of different ways scammers may try to get your money, but they are always working on new schemes so it is equally as important to keep an ear to the ground regarding the latest scam that is going around. This means you are never going to want to do business with a company that isn't reputable, just to save a few dollars as you are risking all of your savings instead.

False exchanges

While not all cryptocurrency exchanges are going to have the same sterling reputation, most at least strive to serve the public with a genuine service. This is not the case with fraudulent exchanges, however, as they are only ever out to take money from those naïve enough to deal with them in the first place. The fastest way to determine if an exchange is really just a scam is to consider its advertising.

If the exchange is offering to sell ether, or another Ethereum based cryptocurrency, for a flat fee that is lower than the current market price then there is literally no chance that they aren't a scam. Cryptocurrency exchanges are just like any other exchange which means that they work with buyers and sellers to match up transactions. No seller is ever going to sell for less than market value, that's why market value exists in the first place.

Another guaranteed red flag is going to be any exchange that offers to buy your cryptocurrency via PayPal. No true exchange uses PayPal to process its transactions, and with a reputable exchange your cryptocurrency doesn't leave your wallet until the transaction has been processed on the chain directly. These types of scams work by getting your PayPal details and then prompting you to send your ether to the address found on a QR code. Unsurprisingly, once you send out your coins the promised payment never materializes and you won't be able to get in touch with those responsible in any way shape or form. This is why it is always recommended that you sell your cryptocurrency through traditional channels.

False wallets

Spotting a fake wallet can be more difficult than seeing through a fake exchange, simply because they have fewer functions, or because they may even appear to be working as intended most of the time. The scam enters into the equation by including malicious code in the download that will attack your device and send your personal data somewhere you would prefer it not be. Ethereum.org has a list of reputable wallets available for download on several different platforms.

The best way to avoid using a fake wallet is to trust your instincts, especially if anything about the website doesn't seem quite right. A good warning sign is for websites that aren't running a secure protocol or that have a name that is almost the same as a well-known wallet, except slightly different. Regardless of where the software comes from, you are going to want to scan it with some type of virus scanner before you let it loose on your system. You can also check with the ether subreddit to determine if the wallet you are considering is worth your time and if others have already used it successfully.

Go phish

Phishing scams are another common occurrence in the digital space surrounding cryptocurrencies. These types of scams work by convincing you that the scammer is someone in a position of authority, likely working with an exchange you frequent or someone from the Ethereum platform itself. These messages will typically try and get you to visit some website which will then either infect your computer, try to get personal information from you, or both. You will typically find this scam in email form, though it may work via popup add as well.

To combat this type of scam, the first thing you are going to need to do is make an effort not to take the bait from emails that don't seem quite on the level. This can be easier said than done, however, as the scammer may have very well hacked a relevant database and the email could appear legitimate. A good rule of thumb then is to never click links or download attachments from emails whose address you cannot verify. Their hyperlinks may give them away, however, as if you hover over them they will show the URL they are related to which may have not been changed.

You will also always want to verify the email address that you are potentially responding to. While this may be spoofed or otherwise faked, it could very well not be which means you may get the information you are looking for. If you do believe an email is real, never make contact through the email itself, always either reach out to the organization with an email of your own, or call a customer service line. Regardless of whether or not the initial contact was legitimate, responding through secure channels is always a better choice. When it comes to dealing with your trade balance, safe is definitely better than sorry.

If you find yourself bombarded with lots of online advertisements, then it is important to take special care to limit what sites you actually visit when online. The most reliable way to avoid being drawn in by these scams is to be more selective when it comes to clicking on search results. The first few returns on any search is going to be little more than paid advertisements which means it could lead virtually anywhere. Clicking on these ad results will never get you to where you need to be and will only expose you to the types of phishing scams you are trying to avoid. Luckily, this is one type of risk you can avoid completely as long as you stop blindly searching and start entering URLs of your destinations directly.

Ponzi

While the specific details behind a Ponzi scheme is going to vary, the cryptocurrency versions all have one major thing in common. Specifically, they require that you send in your cryptocurrency of choice in order to generate a return on your cryptocurrencies that beats the market average in typically as little as a few weeks' time. They are frequently easy to spot because they work off of a referral system and in most other scenarios you don't get random people talking about a great new deal that you have to see to believe. Likewise, if you come across a site that is trying to get you to recruit your friends then what you are generally dealing with is a Ponzi scheme. If you aren't sure if something is too good to be true then it probably is, if you just want to make sure, check out the Ethereum subreddit.

Stay out of the pool

Mining pools, as previously mentioned, are groups of individuals who get together to mine blocks. The more prominent ones have also been known to take on their own investors. Investing in a mining pool generates shares, just as if you were investing in a stock. The mining pool then uses this money to increase their infrastructure and, ultimately, the number of blocks they can successfully mine. This is all well and good if you invest in a legitimate mining pool, but if you invest in one that is fraudulent, you will ultimately lose out in the end. One of the most difficult parts about this scam is that if it is succeeding then you won't have any reason to think anything is wrong. You will receive regular dividends from your investment, but these won't be profits in a traditional sense, rather it will be the fees paid by other investors, shuffled around and around as long as possible.

Matthew Connor

Eventually, however, the returns will slow and then stop all together as potential investors start to catch wind of the scam before being sucked in. This is why it is important to listen to your instincts and check into the relevant details when it comes to determining if anyone has had any issues with the mining pool so far. If you have come across a new pool that is genuinely on the level then they might not have much of a record one way or the other but at least you will be able to weed out those that have already proven to be predatory.

When determining your options, you are also going to need to be aware of various details that a pool should be able to provide. This includes things like details about what blockchain cluster they mine from and if they distribute hash rate via a best-use method. You will also want to be aware of any terms limiting total hash rate as legitimate pools are always going to have limits because required hardware is very expensive and it is always made to order so deployment isn't immediate. Fake services do not impose any limits, likely because they are not doing any actual mining in the first place.

Despite the fact that this scam can seem relatively harmless as long as you are one of the ones making money, it is important to keep in mind that the good times never last. A sign that things are coming to an end is when the pool starts to decrease its rates as a last-ditch effort to squeeze as much money out of the scam as possible. The only thing they care about are profits so you can bet that any and every effort will be made to keep things going before the pool suddenly shuts down unexpectedly. These types of scams can last for years or more, depending on how successful they are to start.

Another good way to tell the fakes from the true mining pools is via their endorsements from a vendor that is registered by ASIC. These vendors are responsible for a majority of the mining machines utilized by mining pools and they are eager to send along a certification logo or a blog post mentioning it as it is free advertising for them and reinforces the notion that their name means quality. If the mining pool you are considering can't provide proof of their ASIC endorsement you will likely want to think twice about them.

Similarly, the mining pool should also be able to easily provide proof of the hardware they run in their data center. If this information isn't readily available on their website then you should be able to get a hold of it by request. Regardless of the response that you receive when you ask for these details, your request is a reasonable one and a company can't provide these details is one you do not want to be involved with.

Investment tips

While investing in ether is as easy as finding the right exchange and making a few trades, investing successfully is a different process entirely. The following are several tips that can make the process more successful for you in the long-term.

Treat it like any other commodity

When it comes to investing, cryptocurrencies aren't that different from other commodities. Both are used for more than one thing, in this case ether is used to power a wide variety of decentralized applications and is also used for speculative purposes, while base metals are used for industrial projects, precious metals are used in the construction of jewelry etc. As such, it is important to ensure that the cryptocurrency you invest in is going to be one that is going to generate value in the real world, which is a test that ether passes with flying colors.

Consider usage rates

Currently, all the cryptocurrencies on the market today have a market cap of about $60 billion. This puts them in the same league as companies like Coca Cola, Boeing and Tesla. What makes this number important is that real world usage has so far gone hand in hand when it comes to increasing market usage which means that it is unlikely that any cryptocurrency, or ether specifically, is going to be going away anytime soon. This means that while the day to day market is still extremely volatile, investing in ether is a viable long-term investment.

The current numbers are being seen despite the fact that less than 25 percent of Americans can explain what a blockchain is while only 2 percent use one on a regular basis. Compared to the market cap, these numbers are extremely encouraging as they show that the usage rates have literally nowhere to go but up. These numbers are exceedingly important as, regardless of the plans for investment, the more people who use them on a regular basis the more profitable they are going to be in the long-term. Additionally, a continuous increase in users will eventually even out the issue they currently have when it comes to pricing bubbles which means investors will eventually not need to worry about prices dropping off dramatically.

Market cycle

The market cycle is a type of pattern that all investments follow sooner or later. Being aware of the cycle will allow you to pick out the current point the market is at with a given asset and act accordingly. The market cycle begins moving in a strong upward direction with a period of optimism, followed by thrill and then peaks at euphoria before moving downward through anxiety, denial, fear and depression before bottoming out at panic. It will then eventually start to rise again, moving through depression, hope and relief before making it back to optimism.

While bitcoin has already been through the full cycle once, after reaching a low point during the crash of 2014, ether is still currently in the optimism stage which means there is still plenty of time for astute investors to take advantage of the fact. Analysts say that it could likely continue in this stage for as long as five more years before reaching the euphoria stage and beginning to decline. Perhaps not coincidentally, five years is about the time that they anticipate it will take for the market to reach a saturation point with cryptocurrency as a whole.

While you are going to want to keep the current state of the market in mind, you are also going to need to realize that much like the dotcom boom from 20 years ago, more than 80 percent of all of the cryptocurrencies on the market today are unlikely to last through the period of market saturation. The Ethereum has a better chance of surviving than most, simply because it has already found a niche for itself and it is also a platform that countless other cryptocurrencies and smart contracts already run on. Investing in it is a better choice than throwing your money at a fly by night cryptocurrency that may very well not be around in a year or less.

Chapter 8: The Future of Ethereum

When it comes to taking advantage of all that the Ethereum offers the blockchain space, a majority of the current usage cases only utilize its ability to transmit financial data. Many of the Ethereum apps that are currently in development, however, are going to expand the blockchain paradigm significantly.

Some of the projects that are currently in development as of the summer of 2017 include:

Blockstream

Blockstream is actually a company that is currently working on a variety of projects. The most important of these is tasked with increasing the speed of cryptocurrency based projects that work with smart contracts. The company recently saw an influx of more than $50 million during a round of series A funding that is being put to work enhancing protocol strength while also funding the completion of several projects including the Lightning Network which will help to speed up smaller blockchain transactions, making everyday usage of cryptocurrencies more likely.

Aeternity

This project is trying to figure out a way to make it easier for the Ethereum platform as a whole to scale its blockchain processes and thus increase transaction speeds even more. It is striving to generate a network that would handle all of the smart contracts separately from the primary blockchain functions, increasing transaction speeds in the process. The contracts that use this secondary network would only come into contact with the primary blockchain at points where verification of transactions was directly required.

ContentKid

This is a unique way of utilizing blockchains in ways that disrupts current payment formulas. ContentKid works by purchasing subscription time to various services such as Hulu or Netflix and then renting out the time in short bursts to interested consumers. Thus, allowing users legal access to a wide variety of content in daily or even hourly bursts rather than in via a traditional monthly or yearly model. The technology behind it is based on a blockchain that provides users with access as needed by automatically completing relating deductions based on time spent to provide a fluid connection to the desired content.

Blockphase

This is a blockchain based tool that helps to enforce copyright infringement for content in the augmented reality, 360-degree video and virtual reality genres. Users are then able to add their content to the Blockphase blockchain which then searches the internet for instances of infringement on a constant basis. This allows users to store and manage their copyrights more easily and decreases the likelihood of intellectual theft, freeing them to create as opposed to having to actively protect their work.

Future uses

Legal work

Smart contracts are already making their way into usage in conjunction with traditional contracts. They make it easier to enact all of the legalese back and forth that is outlined in most contracts when it comes to determining the timing and specifics behind certain actions. Smart contracts cut through all this red tape and automate the things that need to happen once certain external factors are met. In theory, if this practice continues to become more common, there will be less a need for this type of boilerplate content in contracts at all as this could all be handled automatically in the blockchain.

Financial services

The financial service industry is already taking direct steps to make Ethereum a part of all infrastructure moving forward. The Enterprise Ethereum Alliance is racing towards a scenario where the Ethereum platform houses a secondary blockchain that is specifically tailored to the needs of the financial and other industrial sectors. Additionally, smart contracts are going to continue to see an increase in use when it comes to managing workflow and a variety of approval processes that are inherent in processes such as trade clearing and the generation of settlements. Smart contracts will also be used when it comes to determining coupon payments amounts and in the generation of bonds at the point of expiration.

Smart contracts are also starting to see use in the payment of insurance claims after a specific set of binary factors have been met or avoided. With additional refinement, this type of smart contract would essentially be able to take insurance adjusters out of the system completely. The need for personal assessment would be minimized as smart cars would be able to relay all possible data directly to the insurance blockchain to ensure that facts would always hold sway. Insurance companies would also be able to increase or decrease rates automatically based on predetermined driver statistics.

Healthcare

In the field of healthcare, smart contracts are already making headway when it comes to increasing the ways in which patients and their data stay connected. Preliminary usage results from hospital testing indicates that linking patients and their charts together via a blockchain would decrease the likelihood of clerical errors by as much as 40 percent, with that number increasing even more if a serious emergency is thrown into the mix.

Furthermore, apps are currently in development that will theoretically connect individuals to their health information, automatically based on social security information so that it will automatically follow you throughout your life. This would mean no more transferring medical records from one doctor to another of having to track down old x-rays for one reason or another, everything would always be readily available at the press of a button.

The Ethereum platform is also being put to use for potentially tracking medical studies with those in the study having their data transferred automatically for collection and then automatically paying them for their time when the study comes to an end. Perhaps unsurprisingly, a version of this same technology is also on its way to a wide variety of personal internet devices such as those that track fitness goals, except they will soon gain the ability to dole out rewards accordingly.

Increase the adoption of electric cars

Tesla is allegedly working with the Ethereum platform to develop a means of utilizing the blockchain to allow those with electric vehicles to pull up to charging stations and plug in without having to manually enter any type of payment or identification information whatsoever. Each car will be linked to a specific smart contract that will be linked to a bank account and monitor the consumption of energy of the vehicle and charge the account accordingly.

Clerical tasks

Work is already being done to put smart contracts to work updating and correlating clerical information based on a wide variety of different indicators. They will even have the ability to release specific information after the proper digital signatures have been received. Along these same lines, the technology is poised to revolutionize the shipping industry as supply chain movement of all sorts will soon be clearly visible in a chain that is automatically updated as products move from place to place. Payment will also be handled through the blockchain after the products reach a predetermined location. The same process will handle bills of lading, credit and promise payments.

As the usage rate among manufactures grows, the history of every single product that you receive will grower longer and more detailed until you are able to track the path everything took from the manufacturer straight to your doorstep. Blockchain technology even has the potential to streamline the way voting takes place by allowing for the validation of votes beyond the shadow of a doubt in a process so easy and secure it makes the current voting system look like a travesty.

Governmental oversight

The federal government has been concerned about the level of anonymity that is provided by the blockchain process for several years, since it became apparent that criminals were using bitcoin to launder money, as well as commit various illicit activities. As cryptocurrencies become more mainstream, it is only natural that the FBI, DHS, FCEN and the SEC are all starting to give cryptocurrency the attention it deserves.

This scrutiny began to increase in 2013 when the FCEN first decided that exchanges that focus on cryptocurrency are just like any other money service business which means they have to play by the same rules. DHS quickly followed this up by freezing the accounts of the largest cryptocurrency exchange in the world. This eventually lead to a 2017 ruling which denied bitcoin an official cryptocurrency exchange trading fund. A review of this denial is currently making its way through the system.

This leaves cryptocurrency in a bit of an place as the increasing government scrutiny has led to additional levels of checks and balances that were never supposed to be applied to the blockchain in the first place. Furthermore, with the rapidly increasing user base, it will only be a matter of time before it reaches a true saturation point, which will bring about all sorts of issues itself. If these potential issues aren't dealt with before the saturation point is reached, it is unlikely that they ever truly will. If there is hope for cryptocurrency to eventually become just another part of the incumbent financial system then it is going to need to find a way to remain true to itself, while also becoming complex enough to meet the needs of everyone who is going to need to use it. It will also need to find a way to be simple enough to use that everyone who is going to want to use it, will be able to.

Conclusion

Thank you for making it through to the end of **Ethereum: Ultimate Guide to BlockchainTechnology, Cryptocurrency and Investing in Ethereum** , let's hope it was informative and able to provide you with all of the tools you need to achieve your goals, whatever it is that they may be. Just because you've finished this book doesn't mean there is nothing left to learn on the topic, expanding your horizons is the only way to find the mastery you seek.

While you can bet that all types of investment require that you make learning a habit in order to find true success, becoming a lifelong learner in the cryptocurrency market is more important than most. Despite the fact that Ethereum is one of the most stable blockchain platforms available today, it is still nascent technology that could very well start falling apart tomorrow. While this is unlikely to be the case, the point is, unless you are actively keeping up with the latest dirt on the market, you have no real way of knowing for sure.

This should be an easy task as the Ethereum platform, and indeed all cryptocurrency, currently stands at a truly historic point in time and one that will definitely be pointed to in the future as the time when the concept of money started to become truly digital. The usage statistics don't lie, more people are using cryptocurrency every day and it isn't a question of if it is going to reach a point where it will become mainstream, it is a question of when. With this in mind then, it is clear that you have a choice, find the way in which you can profit from this emergent technology or let the opportunity pass you by and miss out on getting in on the ground floor of the technology that is already being called the most important invention since the internet.

Check out other Books by Matthew Connor

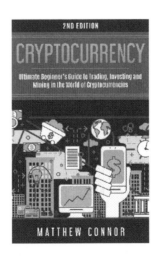

One Final Thing...

Did You Enjoy and Find This Book Useful?

If you did, please let me know by leaving a review on AMAZON. Reviews lets Amazon knows that I am providing quality material to my readers. Even a few words and rating would go a long way. I would like to thank you in advance for your time.

If you didn't, please shoot me an email at matthewconnor@bmccpublishing.com and let me know what you didn't like. I maybe able to change or update it.

Lastly, if you have any feedback to improve the book, please email me. In this age, this book can be a living book. It can be continuously improved by feedback provided by readers like you

About The Author

Matthew Connor is a financial technology analyst and a self-taught computer programmer that currently lives in New York City. After graduating from Princeton University with an MS in Computer Science, Matt is currently working for a Fortune 500 company in Manhattan, NY. Matt is passionate about numbers and likes to analyze data to find trends and patterns. Having made his 1st million from investing in Bitcoin, Matt believes cryptocurrencies will revolutionize the world within the next 10 years. Therefore, he is setting out to share what he had learned so others can also get ahead start too. During his spare time, Matt enjoys hiking, reading, and cooking exotic recipes.

Printed in Great Britain
by Amazon